W9-CEI-153

Persian Cats

by Meredith Dash

Visit us at www.abdopublishing.com

Published by Abdo Kids, a division of ABDO, P.O. Box 398166, Minneapolis, Minnesota 55439.

Copyright © 2015 by Abdo Consulting Group, Inc. International copyrights reserved in all countries. No part of this book may be reproduced in any form without written permission from the publisher.

Printed in the United States of America, North Mankato, Minnesota.

032014

092014

 PRINTED ON RECYCLED PAPER

Photo Credits: AP Images, Shutterstock, Thinkstock

Production Contributors: Teddy Borth, Jennie Forsberg, Grace Hansen

Design Contributors: Dorothy Toth, Renée LaViolette, Laura Rask

Library of Congress Control Number: 2013952421

Cataloging-in-Publication Data

Dash, Meredith.

Persian cats / Meredith Dash.

  p. cm. -- (Cats)

ISBN 978-1-62970-011-3 (lib. bdg.)

Includes bibliographical references and index.

1. Persian cats--Juvenile literature.   I. Title.

636.8--dc23

        2013952421

Table of Contents

Persian Cats

Persian cats are beautiful. They also have sweet personalities.

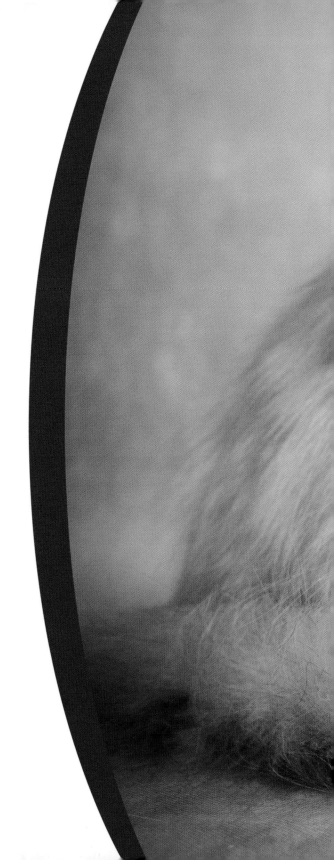

5

Persian cats have long, shiny coats. Brushing them daily will keep their coats healthy.

Persian cats come in

many different colors.

9

Persian cats have very round, flat faces. They have small noses.

11

Persian cats have small ears and large, round eyes.

Persian cats have short, strong legs. Their tails are short and thick.

Persian cats are not jumpers or climbers. You usually will not find them in high places.

Personality

Persian cats prefer a **calm environment**. However, they can get along with children and dogs.

19

Persian cats love the **company** of others. They are happy to sit near you or play a game.

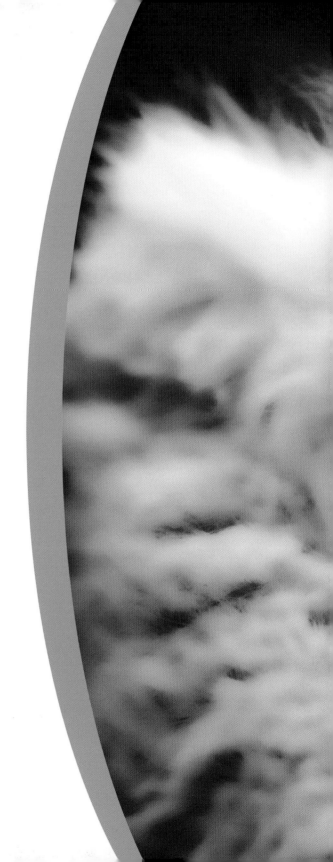

More Facts

- Persians are one of the most popular cat breeds in the United States.

- A Persian cat's eye color will depend on its coat color.

- Some Persian cats' eyes can be two different colors!

Glossary

calm – not showing or feeling anger, or other emotions.

company – being with another or others.

environment – everything that surrounds and affects a living thing.

healthy – in good health.

shiny – bright and glossy.

Index

abdokids.com

Use this code to log on to abdokids.com and access crafts, games, videos and more!

Abdo Kids Code:
CPK0113